Being Me

My Moments in Poetry

Nat Dorléans

Dedicated to my family near and far

Printed in the United States of America

Publisher's Cataloging-in-Publication data

ISBN 978-1-7355296-3-9

This collection of poems are my feelings and thoughts put on paper during a very peculiar time in my life. The poems were written in 1997-1998, 2002, and again in 2007. During that time, I realized the importance of taking care of my mental health. And how my relationships and experiences shaped who I became and who I was becoming.

Table of Contents

1.	Who Am I	7
2.	A Mother of 25 Years	8
3.	Children of the Future	9
4.	2 Crazy Birds	10
5.	The Mother of Christian	11
6.	The 25th Anniversary	12
7.	My Impression of You	13
8.	Family	14
9.	What Does It Mean to be a WOMAN	15
10.	A Tribute to My Parents	16
11.	"Why Do you Love Me" you Asked	17
12.	Duvalier	18
13.	Believe in Yourself	19
14.	All My Life	20
15.	Children of Africa	21
16.	Beautiful Sisters	22
17.	NATHANIEL	23
18.	Missing You	24
19.	Drugs	25
20.	Divorce	26
21.	I am Falling for Your Too	27
22.	November 2nd	28
23.	My Soldier	29

Who Am I

Who am I?
I am a Woman.
I am Black.
I am Haitian.
I am an Intellectual.
I am Lovable.
I am everything and anything I want to be.
Understanding that the real me
Is simply not what you see but the Unseen.
I am a link in the Universe; in Nature
That connects the past, present. and future.
I am a spiritual force that creates a pathway to the impossible and to the light.
I continue to be more than an Intellectual , Black, Haitian Woman who loves
unconditionally.
But more importantly, I am the spirit or the life that grants everything possible.

 11/1997

7

A Mother of 25 Years

For 50 years, YOU walked the Earth
Filled with the memories of the past
And the hopes of the future
As a child you roamed in search of dreams to fulfill h your mind
Dreams of who you are and who you will become
Dreams of becoming a Mother
The mother of Philippe, Nathalie, and David
A mother who has given to her children all the dreams and desires she possess
For 25 priceless years, you have been our mother
The One we turn to for nurturing, care, and support
Or for a new pair of shoes
Thank you!
In your actions, Mommy, we feel your love and your hopes to elevate us to Higher Ground
You are a special mother because of you persevere
Without perseverance, there could not be Philippe, David, or Nathalie
Thanks, mommy, for being who you are
Strong and Powerful!

 05/1997

Children of the Future

(a dedication to all children)

We are the Children of the Future
Full of beauty, hopes, and dreams
To make the world better
And to accomplish all things
We have faith and confidence in myself to be what we want to be
And be able to understand everything that we see

11/1997

9

2 Crazy Birds

There once were two Crazy Birds
That were inseparable
And lived in their own worlds
The Smiles, hugs, and kisses that they once exchanged
And late night romances they cherished
Still Remains mysteriously untouched
Despite society's desire to perish
Their memories and dreams
And Love

There are two Crazy Birds
Who must magically find their way
To each other
Through the Ribbons in the Sky
If they are to remain
Crazy & Bird

  11/7/1997

10

The Mother of Christian

She is in search of meanings and hopes
To Her God in Heaven
She dreams to see her child elevate
To the grounds above
And become one of God's children
A Mother of 10 years
Everyday prays for the health of her child
Mentally, Physically, and Spiritually
She longs and awaits the days
When he becomes a scientist, pastor, or comedian
Or the day when he takes his vows
She strives and works hard to provide him
With nurturance, love, care, and support
So she truly is special
To give to her child
All her priceless dreams and desires
And he thanks her for being who she is
Strong and Powerful!!!

05/1997

11

The 25th Wedding Anniversary
(A dedication to my parents, Leo and Jacqueline)

I know not why you marry
was it love, comfort, loneliness, or was it an accident
I asked myself "Why"
Because I no longer see the happiness in your eyes; all I see is regret and sadness
The wasted years, memories, and disappointments that you no longer want to cherish
So do you marry for commitment and obligation

Now it is your 25th anniversary
What are you to say about marriage
Is it love; It is love
A love far beyond our imagination
It is a love that surpasses the human body
A love of the spirits in the mind
A love that is accepting of The what is and what is not
and the ability to conceive beyond
I now see the happiness in your eyes and there is no more regret and sadness
The Wasted years, memories, and disappointments
Were the roads to truth and understanding that you can now cherish
You are now no longer afraid to love
And it took 25 years to realize that such Treasures comes deeper
Then what you can see and touch
It is about spirituality and freedom of the mind
It is about love after 25 years of marriage

2/23/1998

12

My Impression of You
(Dedicated to this Haitian Philosopher)

You entered the room and my heart skipped a beat
I began to shudder from my head to my feet
Not because of the beauty that defines your face
Rather because of the overwhelming feelings that you place
In Me
Truly
Feelings of things that I have only imagined
But through your smile and words I know that it could all happen
To be free like the birds through your spiritual force
I recognize my power to have a choice
I was moved by the spirit of you
That I began to feel and be in contact with what is true
Your presence, your movements
Your essence, your elements
Your spirit which allows for my body to be elevated
To another level ,I listen to your words, and I am emancipated
Thank you for recognizing and redefining me
For I realized that who we are now may not be what we were meant to be

03/1998

Family
(Dedication to my family who are in Haiti, Canada, and throughout the U.S. and World)

I am sorry
I am unable to see and hold you
The distance between us degenerates our relationship
To a quick phone call
But I have you in my mind
The memory of your face, laughter, and love
Is ingrained in me
I can never forget you
Not only because you are my flesh and blood
But because you are a part of me
I recognize and cherish you
Through my prayers and thoughts
You are my family and must always be remembered

  03/03/1998

What Does It Mean to be a WOMAN?

What does it mean to be a WOMAN?

Does it mean being biologically different? Does it mean being socially different ?

Having breast; having a vagina; having children; having long hair; wearing lipstick

Being caring nurturing pure week inferior passive dependent indecisive loving

What does it mean to be a woman being a WOMAN?

Being a WOMAN Means Understanding...

That she is unique from other creatures

Yet one with nature in the cosmic world

WOMAN means understanding herself and those around her

Being a WOMAN Means Responsibility...

For her actions, thoughts, body, and feelings

By enlightening Her Mind Body Soul

WOMAN means being responsible for herself and those around her

Being a WOMAN Means Respect...

To have a positive self-image (Mind Body Soul)

And acknowledging her existence, individuality, and voice

WOMAN means respecting herself and those around her

Being a WOMAN Means Spirituality...

Recognizing that there is more to being a WOMAN than what she has been taught

WOMAN means being one with herself and those around her

Being a WOMAN means everything and anything she wants it to be

04/25/1998

15

A Tribute to My Parents

Thank you to my ancestors
Who first created civilization
With their communities, philosophies, sociologies, and psychologies
You are the queens and kings of my world
And with you I am able to achieve and succeed
By believing and trusting myself and you
You freed me from oppression
Introduced me to freedom
Freedom to understand
Freedom to think
Freedom to live my life as I see it not as others have me be
I want to thank you
African King and Queen
Toussaint, Dessaline
Cloraine, Odette
Lelio, Josias
Leo, Jacqueline
For your guidance to freedom
Your love, strength, encouragement, and spirituality
Helped me to accomplish my dreams to reality so I can now conquer the world

03/03/1998

"Why Do you Love Me" you Asked

I love you because of the way you look at me

With a tender stare that warms my heart

I love you because of the way you make me feel

Like the most important person in the world

I love you because of the way you care about me

Like a man does a woman

I love you because of the way you console me

By making everything better

I love you because of the way you touch me

With your gentle hands and passionate lips

I love you because of the way you protect me

From harm and pain

I love you because of the way you cater to me

Simply, to please me

I love you because of the way you smile at me

So innocently

I love you because of the way you caress me

With so much love and desire

I love you because of the way you walk

With Grace and Ease

I love you because of the way you talk

With confidence in finesse

I love you because of the way you move your body

The right way

I love you because of the way your body pleases mine

Perfectly

I love you because you are the best thing that has happened to me

04/28/1998

Duvalier

You are a Revolutionary
Like the Brothers before You
You opened the door to a new world
A World that is Accepting of people that are not "acceptable"
Please like ME
Poor, Black, Nappy-headed, Haitian, African ME
You gave me the opportunity to excel
Be deconstructing the forces that kept me uneducated and ignorant
I, thank you for not following the status quo
Rather for believing in me
The Haitian People, the black Woman and the Black Man

You are a Revolutionary
And like all revolutionaries
You are ahead of your time
You are criticised and chastised by your beneficiaries
For wanting to free your people
From the hands of tyranny
You sacrificed many to ensure the survival of your raced
By putting Black people in the positions of leadership
You are a Hero
For showing me that everything is Possible
I will help Haiti- My Country

03/05/1998

Believe in Yourself

Believe in Yourself
Children of Africa
You are beautiful with your unique coarse hair
And darker skin
A perfect creation
Children of Africa
Be Proud
Be proud of your individuality and creativity
Be proud of your intellect and you gain respect
For yourself
And for your sisters and brothers

Believe in Yourself
Children of Africa
Believe in the Force
That has made you
Who and what you are
A lively in entity
Full of Beauty
Hopes, Dreams, and Desires
To OVERCOME
Believe in yourself, Children of Africa, because you hold the key

07/13/1998

All My Life

All my life, I searched for someone like you,... Someone to love me even when times are blue

Someone who is not afraid to share his love ...By spreading his peaceful wings like a dove

In the sky ...You are high

Higher than the material world

And more precious than a shining pearl

So I Look to You For Comfort

especially when I am hurt

Let us forget about the past

And focus on making the present last

Afterall, our we are a match

That others long to catch

But I am never going to let you go

Even when times are low

Because we are a team

Full of Dreams

All my life, I searched for someone like you

Someone I could talk and be true to

Someone Like You, the best

Full of finesse

You are the man for me

Though sometimes, I cannot see

But I pray to the Lord above

To cherish us with love

And I continue to pray ..Everyday

So our love can grow strong ..And long

Most importantly, I pray for spirituality ..So I can be in love with you for all eternity

04/20/1998

Children of Africa

Good day, Children of Africa
Lift up your voices and sing
To the spirits of your ancestors
Praise them as they praised you
For a continuity
And the continuance of our soul

Good day, Children of Africa
SHOUT! LAUGH! DANCE!
To your freedom and livelihood
Given to you by your ancestors
With their blood, voice, life, and strength

Good day, Children of Africa
And live
The life inherited to you
By the Queens, Kings, Slaves, Leaders, and Warriors of Africa
Believe
In yourself and your ancestors
And know that you are FREE

  07/14/1998

Beautiful Sisters

Beautiful sisters...
Listen! My sisters!
You are beautiful
Just the way you are
You were created Perfect and Flawless
With your curly coarse hair
Shiny brown eyes
Luscious full lips
Cute brown nose
And luminous shades of brown
Yes! My sisters!
You are beautiful
With your afros and your braids
And different sizes and shapes
Sisters!
Be proud of what you look like and who you are
Perfect and Beautiful

07/14/1998

NATHANIEL
Nathaniel means gift from God
Born on June 5th 2002

Have you ever looked into the eyes of your baby and asked yourself
Is this for real?
"I have participated in creating this precious, fearless, miraculous joy"
That is what I thought when I looked at you
A Perfect Creation from God
A gift given to me by God to cherish and nourish

06/05/2002

Missing You

I close my eyes
And I see your smile
Now I am missing you
And learning to be me without you

 *2003*

Drugs

The Birth of the Destruction of Man
The Source of the Escape
The Rise of Selfishness
The Fall of Family

 2003

Divorce

Who knew I'd be in front of the judge today
Signing part of my life away
You and I were once a great pair Crazy In Love
But now that flew away like a dove
Who knew I'd be standing here unable to budge
Talking about us in front of the judge
The 2nd of February asking for divorce
Because our path is no longer on course
I say goodbye to you my dear
And our love in its 13th year

  02/2005

26

I'm Falling for You Too

On December 3rd 2006,
you said that it's me that you miss
On July 5th of 2005,
I caught your eye
Not knowing today
That I'd feel this way
A way that is true
When I look at you
An African king
Who loves with his whole being
A love for your daughter
That grows each day stronger
A love for a son
That can never be undone
You tell me this day
That you possibly may
Be falling for me
And all I could see
Is I'm falling for you too

12/06/2006

November 2nd

This is the day to show our worth
Worth of unity, strength, pride and justice
Who said it couldn't be done!
You?
Not me.
If we believe, we can achieve
November 2nd is a day to not purchase anything
But to stand up for all of human being

 10/25/2007

My Soldier

"I am a soldier", you say to me

Because of your strength, courage, pride, and dignity

To fight for what you believe in

No tears, no weaknesses, no insecurities, no fears

"I am a soldier", you say to me

But all I want to do is care, protect, defend, and befriend you

Despite your armor and weapons

In protective gears to shelter you from the world

"You are my Soldier" I say to you

Who is in need of tender, loving, care

So trust, open, and let your guards down and allow for another Soldier to fight for you

 10/26/2007

About the Author

Nat Dorléans is native of Port-au-Prince, Haiti and has been in the U.S. since the age of 8. She is a licensed mental health therapist. She is currently living in Atlanta, GA with her 18 y/o son.

www.ingramcontent.com/pod-product-compliance
Lightning Source LLC
Chambersburg PA
CBHW021922040426
42448CB00007B/876